BARBARA JOHNSON

Humor Me, I'm Your Mother!

THOMAS NELSON
Since 1798

W Publishing Group books may be purchased in bulk for educational, business, fund-raising, or sales promotional use. For information, please email SpecialMarkets@ThomasNelson.com.

Published by W Publishing Group, a division of Thomas Nelson, Inc., P.O. Box 141000, Nashville, TN 37214.

Unless otherwise indicated, Scripture quotations used in this book are from The Holy Bible, New International Version (NIV). Copyright © 1973, 1978, 1984, International Bible Society. Used by permission of Zondervan. Other Scripture quotations are from these sources: The Holy Bible, New Century Version (NCV), copyright © 1987, 1988, 1991 by Word Publishing, a division of Thomas Nelson, Inc. Used by permission. All rights reserved. The Living Bible (TLB), copyright © 1971 by Tyndale House Publishers, Wheaton, IL. Used by permission. New American Standard Bible ® (NASB), © 1960, 1962, 1963, 1968, 1971, 1972, 1973, 1975, 1977, 1995 by the Lockman Foundation. Used by permission.

Many of the stories, jokes, and quips included in this volume have been contributed to the author as unidentified clippings or Internet postings, and although diligent attempts have been made to identify the material's origin, in many cases this was impossible. When these items are specified as source unknown, the author claims no rights or ownership. Selected items in *Humor Me, I'm Your Mother* have previously appeared in the author's earlier books published by Word Publishing and W Publishing Group. While the author's personal experiences related here are true, details may have been changed to protect identities or exaggerated to accommodate the author's great love of laughter. Some anecdotes are composites of the author's or her acquaintances' experiences or products of their imaginations.

Library of Congress Cataloging-in-Publication Data

Johnson, Barbara (Barbara E.)
    Humor me, I'm your mother / Barbara Johnson.
      p. cm.
    Includes bibliographical references.
    ISBN 1-4002-7808-2
    1. Motherhood--Humor. 2. Child rearing--Humor. I. Title: Humor me, I am your mother.
II. Title.
HQ759.J618 2006
306.874'3--dc22
2006005143

Printed in the United States of America

06 07 08 09 10 WOR 9 8 7 6 5 4 3 2 1

Dedicated to
laughter-loving moms
who need a little lift.

Contents

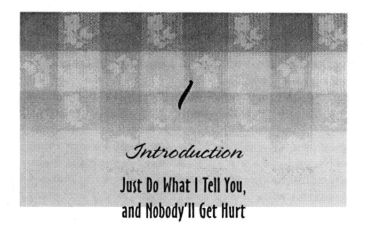

Introduction

Just Do What I Tell You,
and Nobody'll Get Hurt

*S*ome friends were comparing their parenting notes, laughing as they admitted the things they were dismayed to hear coming out of their mouths: the same ridiculously ominous threats and warnings their own parents had said to them a couple of decades earlier. These moms had sworn they would never say such things to their own kids, but the words came tumbling out anyway, uninvited.

"If I have to stop this car, you are really gonna get it!" one mother confessed to yelling into the back of the minivan. Her own mother had made that threat to her and her brother a million times, she said, "usually with one hand on the steering wheel and the other one swinging wildly across the backseat of the station wagon while my brother and I ducked and dodged to stay out of the way."

She didn't remember her mother ever actually stopping the car, "but she slammed on the brakes a few times to make us think she was going to." Now this mom admits she yells "the same things my mom yelled, and since my kids are now wearing seat belts (which my brother and I never did), I usually manage to connect with one or two of them as my arm flails around back there."

"Don't make me come up there!" another mom said, squinting her eyes and pointing her finger up an imaginary stairway.

"If you do that one more time, you're gonna wish you hadn't," a third mom chimed in. "And also . . . , 'You'll put your eye out with that thing!'

Yes, we moms have inherited the words, and we know how to use them, giving us the ability to instantly go from sweetness-and-light to hormonal monster. As one mom laughingly put it, "I am connected straight from heaven to hell, and I can change in a flash. It's a trait I inherited from my mother."[1]

As the mother of four sons, I'm fluent in those warnings, proclamations, and other mother-speak messages that have echoed down the world's hallways and highways for generations. I've been known to spew out a few of them myself. (Although, since I was a sweet and perfect child, I rarely heard my own mother utter such words to precious little *me*. Really. You believe that, don't you?)

Actually, I probably sound like a strict disciplinarian when the truth is, there were a few times when I caught my boys in some kind of mischief—and jumped right in to join them. Perhaps you've heard about the time I came home to find the four of them sitting around the kitchen table, flipping spoonfuls of red Jell-O onto the white-painted brick wall. I stood there a minute, taking in the situation, until finally one of the culprits saw me. Then all four of them froze in mid-flip, their eyes wide, their breaths held up in their trembling chests. They were in big trouble, that's for sure, and they knew it. For starters, they were going to have to scrub that wall and get every morsel of red Jell-O out of every crack, crevice, and crinkle of the bricks and mortar.

But in the meantime, I thought, it *did* look like fun. And since they were going to have to clean the wall anyway, I sat down at the table, pulled the bowl of Jell-O my way, and joined in the mayhem. We flipped every jiggling glob of that Jell-O onto the wall, giggling and shrieking with every blast. We laughed like crazy people—and *then* came the mother-speak: "Well, that was fun! And now . . . if you know what's good for you"—I smiled knowingly as I stood up to leave the kitchen—"you'll get this mess cleaned up fast, before your dad gets home. Have fun!"

"It's not fair. Just as I'm turning into my mother,
she gets to turn into a grandma."

Motherhood: Dreams, Screams, and Adventures

When you have four boys, as we did, there are certain mother-speak phrases, often questions, that seem to be repeated on a daily—if not an hourly—basis:

"What did I tell you about leaving the refrigerator door open?"

"*WHO* did this?"

"*WHY* did you do that?"

"Didn't I tell you *NOT* to do that?"

"If only you would *DO* what I tell you . . ."

And then there's the ultimate phrase in mother-speak: "*BECAUSE I SAID SO, THAT'S WHY!*"

Ah, motherhood. Isn't it fun? And exhausting—oh, so exhausting.

We put our heart and soul into rearing, teaching, protecting, and loving these little gifts from God, and in return they seem to put every ounce of their boundless energy into either driving us crazy or charming our socks off.

We dress up our sweet little bundle of joy in the outfit Grandma sent for that all-important first Christmas picture at the portrait studio. Then we beam proudly as the photographer focuses admiringly on our beautiful child . . . right up until the moment when the picture is actually snapped and the infant erupts in either projectile vomiting, explosive diarrhea—or both, simultaneously.

We wear ourselves out getting our youngsters ready for that all-important first day of kindergarten—then stagger back home from the school or the bus stop, wearily realizing we'll have to repeat this crazy fire-drill of a readiness exercise for *hundreds* of mornings to come.

"Cinderella lived happily ever after until she had kids. After that she was too tired to know if she was happy or not."

During the next thirteen or more years of school we scream encouragement from soccer-field sidelines, sell cookies for the Girl Scouts, make salt maps of Venezuela, clean chewing gum out of hair and pick peanuts out of noses, dissect earthworms for science projects, shampoo the carpet after birthday sleepovers, learn the fastest way to the all-night pharmacy, listen for the door to open as curfew nears, and blink back tears as our babies walk across a stage to accept a diploma or walk down an aisle to marry another mother's child.

Motherhood is an adventure, a white-knuckle thrill ride soothed occasionally by heartwarming moments. It seems that one minute we're new parents just home from the hospital, wondering how on earth we will ever raise this newborn baby—and the next minute we're standing in the driveway, waving good-bye as Junior drives off into the future.

The Great Irony

By the time we've served a few years as mothers, we are *so* smart about parenting; we have valuable experience and tremendous wisdom. Unfortunately, it is just about this time—say, twelve or thirteen years into it—that the people we're trying to parent suddenly seem to lose any interest in listening to us!

This whole business of child rearing would go so much more smoothly if only our children would simply do what we tell them to do. But then, to be honest, it probably wouldn't be nearly as much fun—and it certainly wouldn't be as exciting: no spit-up baby formula on the front of our favorite silk blouse before the big interview, no lipstick masterpieces on the living room walls, no backyard funeral for the goldfish, no thrill-ride trips to the emergency room, no stuffed animals to res-cue from the commode, no baby teeth to dig out of the drain in the bathroom sink, no passionate passages to be refereed during the turbulent teenage years . . .

Without such memories, we wouldn't have nearly as much to laugh about when we look back on our mother-ing years. For example, my friend Ann told me about going to a friend's house one time and finding a wooden door leaning against the wall of the living room. Seeing Ann's raised eyebrows, the friend tossed her head toward her teenage daughter's bedroom. "I told her if she slammed that door one more time it was coming unhinged," the friend explained ruefully.

"I thought you said *you* were coming unhinged!" the daughter, overhearing the conversation, yelled from her now-doorless bedroom. "I didn't know you were gonna take the darn door down. I thought you said *you* were coming unhinged, and so I thought, like, *Hel-loooooo! What else is new?* Mom, seriously. Would you just bring my door back?"

Now, see? You just have to laugh, don't you? And that's the important thing. In my opinion, the choice for active-duty parents is either to laugh—or check into the Home for the Bewildered. (Which is still a possibility in case you start laughing and can't stop. I understand they're considering naming a room there in my honor.)

© 1998 Randy Glasbergen.
www.glasbergen.com

GLASBERGEN

**"This is the perfect watch for mothers.
Every day is 36 hours!"**

Eternally Maternal

I've often said that becoming a parent is like getting a life sentence with no hope of parole. Once we give birth, mothering becomes part of our psyche. The next thing we know, those mother-speak words move into our minds and leak out our mouths, and there's basically nothing we can do to stop them, try as we might.

And they just keep on coming, no matter how old we get. Recently I heard about a sixty-year-old woman whose eighty-five-year-old mother sent her a six-pack of cotton underpants—the style kids today call "granny panties." Inside was a note that said, "Honey, always remember to put on clean underwear every morning. Love, Mama."

This book is about the misadventures of motherhood, those moments of maternal mirth, whenever and wherever they occur, that make us laugh—just as soon as we can stop crying. I've divided this little collection into age groups and included some of my favorite funnies— jokes, cartoons, and stories I've heard, experienced, collected, dreaded, or imagined with the help of my friends. (As one of them says, I never let the *facts* stand in the way of a good story.) So settle back and loosen up anything tight; you're gonna need room to laugh. (I don't know about you, but for me, this just about means being stark naked.) Whether you *are* a mother or you *have* a mother, no matter what age you are or what stage you're in, I hope you'll find joy and laughter in the pages ahead.

"Dad said you got a 24-hour virus . . .
How much time do you have left?"

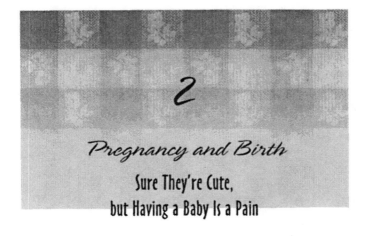

2

Pregnancy and Birth

Sure They're Cute,
but Having a Baby Is a Pain

*W*hat a happy, expectant, jubilant time pregnancy is. Four times I experienced the joys of pregnancy, and each time I loved it.

For about fifteen minutes.

Then I wanted my regular body back.

No, I'm just kidding. There are a lot of good things about being pregnant. One of my favorite things was that, just for a little while, it was my secret alone. First it was just a suspicion: I was a few days late in my cycle, and I began to wonder . . .

Then maybe another month went by, and my suspicions grew stronger. Finally I scheduled a doctor's appointment. The way things worked back then, you generally had to wait a month, or usually two, before you got pretty confident you were not alone in your body. Eventually you went to the doctor's office and donated a urine sample, and then, if you were pregnant, a few days later you would get a call and be told, "The rabbit died."

Well, no, I'm just kidding about that too. They only said that in comedy shows. But back in the "olden days," a rabbit *was* needed if you wanted to know you were pregnant before you actually *looked* pregnant (either that, or you could just wait nine months and see if a baby showed up). The doctor's office would send the urine sample to a lab, the lab would inject the urine into a female rabbit, and a few days later the little bunny would be "examined" to see if she was reacting the way rabbits react when they're injected with the urine of a pregnant woman.

Watching the Dipstick

Back then, this kind of pregnancy test was considered fascinating, modern-day science. Today, when you can dip a stick into a cup of urine and find out instantly whether you're "already a winner," the rabbit test sounds pretty primitive, doesn't it?

Often couples eagerly watch the test's indicator together, peering intently at the stick to see what color it turns or what words or symbols appear so they both know at the same instant whether they are about to become parents. Sometimes, as disgusting as it seems (I mean, it *is* dipped in urine), that little test stick becomes a family artifact, the first item tucked into the baby book. Or it gets slipped into a gift box and presented to the grandma-to-be at Christmastime (let's just hope it's in a plastic bag!).

Maternity clothes are different now too. Today many pregnant gals let it all hang out, wearing tiny little T-shirts and low-slung slacks or skirts so they can proudly display their new condition. Modern celebrities happily pose to let their "bump" be photographed by the national press. Such exhibitions would have been outrageous during my pregnancies. Back then, the main idea was to hide the obvious as long as possible. So we moms-to-be wore big, loose tops that, on windy days, made us look like circus tents that had pulled loose from their moorings and were drifting down the sidewalk.

Some moms-to-be get a little touchy about being touched.

One thing that's probably the same for *all* generations of moms-to-be is our feeling about the "touch factor." Most of us do *not* want strangers—or strange relatives—touching our tummies, whether we hide our protruding shape with enough fabric to rig a sailing ship or choose to wear a revealing bikini in our ninth month. And yet, those hands just keep on reaching out and patting us as though the baby-to-be is a pet Chihuahua. I'll bet fashion designers could make a fortune selling maternity T-shirts imprinted with "Private Property," or "Keep Off!"

Hospital Time

Of course, once we make it to the delivery room, any sense of modesty or privacy we might have clung to during pregnancy goes right out the window, and suddenly it seems like all sorts of people are lining up to look at our most-private parts. In recent months I've even heard about parents who host birth-day parties right in the hospital's maternity ward so that family members, friends, neighbors, and presumably anyone else looking for free food can share in welcoming the new arrival. One advantage to that kind of gathering, I suppose, is that you can throw a party but be excused from any kind of hostessing duties.

To be honest, even if I had to do it over again, I think I would stick with the old way of doing things. Before most of my boys were born, I got some kind of shot and blissfully enjoyed "twilight sleep" through the exciting parts. The exception was with our first son, Tim, who was so eager to make his arrival that he was almost born in the car! Luckily my sister Janet was visiting the day I went into labor. When it became obvious that things were happening too fast for my husband to make it home in time, she nervously drove me to the hospital and dropped me off at the door, then frantically looked for a parking spot while the nurses wheeled me up to the labor-and-delivery floor.

When Janet finally got the car parked and figured out where they had taken me, she rushed to that department, determined to be there for me and hold my hand during the worst of the labor pains. Instead, she was met in the hallway by the doctor, who told her, "It's a boy!"

Really, there couldn't be a much easier way for a woman to have a baby than that—unless scientists could figure out a way to follow seahorses' example and let the dads be the ones who go through pregnancy and birth. I'd love to live long enough to see that happen. As one quipster said, if men got pregnant, natural childbirth wouldn't be nearly as popular!

I read about one recent trend that teaches moms-to-be how to do self-hypnosis to ease them through labor and delivery. The story described a pregnant woman who learned to imagine a light switch on the back of her neck that she could flip, through hypnosis, to switch off the pain as the baby started coming.[1] Reading that story, I couldn't help but think that, klutz that I am, if I tried that technique I would probably manage to short-circuit the imaginary light switch and set myself on fire.

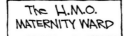

But I didn't need any medications or techniques when Tim was born. As my doctor told me, "You didn't even get a chance to push!"

After a birth as easy as that one, is it any surprise that we quickly decided to have another child? Why, giving birth was downright fun!

Changing Styles
We eventually had three more babies, all boys, and I noticed how our parenting styles changed with each one. The same is true for young couples today. Things change with each additional child. For example, for the first baby, you attend weekly classes and faithfully practice your breathing. With the second baby, you try to keep breathing when you find your two-year-old teetering at the top of the basement stairs. With the third baby, you threaten to hold your breath indefinitely unless the doctor gives you anesthesia to knock you out through the whole third trimester.

Stress-coping strategies also change with each additional child. For instance, with the first baby, you worry so much about the baby's cries that you never put the infant down—you wear her constantly in a baby carrier strapped to your chest. When the second baby cries, you pick him up only when his hysterics threaten to wake up your firstborn. With the third child, you teach your other two kids where to look for the pacifier and how to rewind the baby swing.

Parents' dealings with babysitters also change as

their families grow. The first time you leave your first baby with a sitter, you conduct a two-hour training session then call home four times while you run to the post office. With the second baby, just before you walk out the door you remember to leave an emergency phone number—your neighbor's. With the third baby, you tell the sitter to call only if someone needs stitches, splints, or an ambulance.

Baby activities change too. You take your first infant to baby swim classes, baby aerobics, and baby massage. You take your second baby to infant story hour so you can nap while the story is read. You take your third child to the McDonald's drive-through.

© 2006. Reprinted courtesy of Bunny Hoest and Parade Magazine.

"Your father and I have *always* wanted more children. It's not a reflection on your performance."

And finally, you use your time differently as your mothering management duties increase. You spend hours each day staring adoringly at your precious first infant. With the second baby, you glance in her direction as you race to stop your toddler from trying to climb into the aquarium or drop the cat down the laundry chute. With the third child, you train the dog to guard the baby from his siblings a few hours each day while you hide in the closet.

No matter how many times you've been wheeled into the delivery room, I hope these little giggles will help you chuckle about the start—or maybe the restart—of your years as a mom whose kids know well the sound of their mother's laugher.

Motherhood Mirth

A laughter-loving mother told me she and her husband already had four young sons when their first daughter was born. When her husband came home from the hospital that day and told the boys they had a new baby sister, one of them exclaimed, "Oh, won't Mom be surprised when she gets home!"[2]

☺

There is something about babyness that brings out the softness in people and makes them want to hug and protect this small thing that moves and dribbles and produces what we poetically call poopoo. Even that becomes precious, for the arrival of a baby coincides with the departure of our minds.

—BILL COSBY[3]

Here's how actor Paul Reiser described the birth of his first child: "I remember that my wife cried like a baby. The baby, ironically, cried like an angry woman in her thirties. I cried like a man exactly my age. The three of us cried, and held each other, and cried a little more, and then somebody nice must have packed us up and taken care of everything, because somehow, sometime later, the three of us—now and forever a family—went home."[4]

☺

In an effort to prepare expectant parents for the challenges that lie ahead, many obstetricians' offices have installed parenthood simulators.

☺

God has made me laugh. Everyone who hears about this will laugh with me.

—SARAH, AGED WIFE OF ONE-HUNDRED-YEAR-OLD ABRAHAM,

UPON THE BIRTH OF THEIR SON, ISAAC (GENESIS 21:6 NCV)

3

Newborns and Toddlers

How a Mother Spells Relief: S-L-E-E-P

*Y*ou've brought your bundle of joy home from the hospital, and now maybe you're standing there in the nursery wondering if you really have what it takes to be a mommy. Of course you do! But to help you get ready for what's to come, here are a few fun suggestions for how you can develop the parenting skills you'll need during the next few years.

Financial Preparation: Arrange for direct deposit of your family's paycheck so it's split equally between the nearest grocery store and the pediatrician's office for the next ten years.

Mess-Management Preparation: Smear grape jelly on the living room furniture and curtains. Now plunge your hands into a bag of potting soil, wipe them on the walls, and highlight the smudges with crayons. Rub a half-finished red lollipop through your hair, then lay it on the new carpeting.

Aromatherapy Preparation: Empty a carton of milk onto the cloth upholstery of the family car, park the vehicle in a sunny spot, and leave it to ripen during the month of August.

BABY BLUES   BY RICK KIRKMAN & JERRY SCOTT

Pain-Endurance Preparation: Collect enough small, plastic superhero action figures to fill a fifty-five-gallon drum. (You may substitute thumbtacks or broken glass.) Ask a friend to spread them all over the floors of your house after you've gone to bed, paying special attention to the stairway. Set your alarm for 2 a.m., and when it goes off, rush madly around the dark minefields of your house, trying to figure out where the noise is coming from (the clock? the cordless phone? the baby?), *then* try to remember where you left it. Remember not to scream (you'll wake the baby).

Family-Shopping Preparation: Herd a flock of goats through the grocery store. Always keep all goats in sight, and bring enough money to pay for whatever they eat or destroy.

Aerobic-Agility Preparation: Try to dress the family cat in a small pantsuit, complete with button-up shirt, snap-leg pants, lace-up shoes, and a bow tie while the neighbor's German shepherd barks encouragement from two feet away. (Make sure paramedics are standing by.)

Mealtime Preparation: Sit at the kitchen counter and carefully spoon strained peas and chocolate pudding into a plastic bag. When the bag is completely full, tie a knot to close it, place it on the counter at eye level about a foot from your face, then ask your spouse to smash the bag with an unabridged dictionary.

Attitude Preparation: Have a schoolteacher friend record the sounds of her second-graders scratching their fingernails across a chalkboard. Then fill a small canvas bag with ten pounds of cat litter soaked thoroughly in water. Attach the bag to a tape player with large speakers, and insert the nails-on-chalkboard recording. Beginning at about 8 p.m., hold the bag against your shoulder, play the chalkboard recording at its loudest volume, and waltz around the room with a bumping-and-swooping step, patting the cat litter and making shooshing sounds. Continue for forty minutes, then gently put the bag to bed and turn off the tape player. Repeat hourly until 5 a.m. Then crawl into bed, set the alarm for 6, and then get up and make breakfast while looking cheerful. Repeat for the next five years.

"O.K. sweties. You're all going to need to go naked for just a day or two till Mommy catches up with laundry."

What We Want Most

Now, of course this is all foolishness. Newborns and toddlers would never put their mothers through such ordeals. Not intentionally anyway. Still, many new mothers do find themselves occasionally lapsing into dreamy fantasies of . . . dreaming. Ask most moms at this stage of parenting what they fantasize about, and it's not the Prize Patrol showing up on their doorstep with a bunch of balloons and a check for ten million dollars. What they want most is simply a good night's sleep uninterrupted by crying, screaming, or loud noises related to unpleasant small-body functions.

Of course the first morning you awaken to realize you *have* gotten to sleep through the night, instead of waking refreshed and easing into the day, you'll probably rush into the baby's room to make sure he or she is still alive. We've all done it.

Our youngest son, Barney, was my most demanding baby. During his first few months he was plagued with colic and wanted almost constant attention. I finally had the brilliant idea (if I do say so myself) of putting him on the clothes dryer to sleep. (I'm always careful, when I'm telling this story, to say I put him *on* the dryer, not *in* the dryer.)

I would wrap him snugly in a baby blanket and settle him into a wicker laundry basket, put it on top of the dryer, and set the dryer to run for the full cycle—fifty-eight minutes. Then I would set another timer in the kitchen for a few minutes less so that I could go in and restart the dryer before the cycle ended and the buzzer went off. Barney might be howling his head off, but as soon as he was tucked into his little bed and the dryer's humming vibrations started up, he was snoozing away.

Another mother told me she put her babies to bed in their crib and left the vacuum cleaner running in the hallway. "The sound of that motor whirring away would put them right to sleep," she said. "I wore out three vacuum cleaners just getting my kids to take their naps."

Such tricks work great during the day; while our babies slept to the hum of a household appliance, that other mom and I could get some housework done and tend to the latest mischief our other kids had dreamed up. But nighttime was a different story, since I didn't want to get up every fifty-five minutes to reset the dryer (not to mention my worries that Barney might start thinking the old Maytag was his mother!). Instead, Bill and I took turns walking the floor with the bawling baby. As a result, by the time the sun came up we both looked like characters in *Night of the Zombies*.

Did I mention that motherhood is exhausting? Forgive me if I'm repeating myself. Just thinking back on those nonstop days and excruciating nights makes me tired, even after all these years!

Bleary-Eyed Breakfasts

Maybe you've seen those TV programs that follow medical residents as they work in hospitals for thirty-six hours straight. As they near the end of their shifts, it's a miracle the weary doctors-in-training can find their way to the coffeepot, let alone remove someone's appendix. New moms can experience the same kind of mind-numbing exhaustion, especially nursing moms who are the sole provider of nourishment for their hungry infants. "Sometimes I feel like a human vending machine," one mom said, "except I only dispense one flavor."

One mom who had a new baby when her older children were five and three recalled the problems she endured each morning in her sleep-deprived state as she tried to fix breakfast for her two preschoolers after being up several times during the night with the baby.

THE FAMILY CIRCUS   By Bil Keane

"Let's go ask Mommy for
an ice cream cone."

As picky eaters, her older children had very specific requirements for breakfast. The little boy like "not-burned toast." (Even though the mother had only burned it a few times, the boy always asked for the "not-burned" kind; apparently the incinerated slices she had occasionally served had caused some kind of mental scarring.) His toast had to be cut into triangles and spread with grape jelly, and the only children's chewable vitamin he would even consider was the orange one shaped like Omar the Ogre or some other lovable monster.

The little girl's breakfast order consisted of "cold toast" spread with strawberry preserves and cut into strips.

Cold toast, the mother explained, a little embarrassed,

"is frozen bread. I know it's strange, but I didn't complain. At least I couldn't burn it."

The little girl had to have the purple vitamin pill, the one shaped like Petunia Prissypants, the mother recalled, admitting several years later that she might have forgotten the pills' correct names.

The breakfast orders were specific but not all that complicated really. The problem was that the mom had had no sleep, and at that early morning hour her brain was unable to function properly. So, on more than one morning, she accidentally cut the cold toast into triangles and spread the not-burned toast with strawberry preserves. Even worse, as she dug through the vitamins looking for Omar the Ogre and Petunia Prissypants, she would sometimes zone out completely and be startled awake several minutes later wondering why the tornado siren was going off upstairs and trying to remember the identities of the two miniature people who were peering over the kitchen counter, crying because she had "ruined the toast again."

By the time the woman sorted it all out, she said, the house was in bedlam. The baby's tornado-siren cries had upset the dog, who joined in with loud, pitiful howls, and one time, while she was stumbling around upstairs trying to remember her way to the nursery, the two preschoolers, astutely realizing their mother's mind had gone AWOL, called 911.

It was a little embarrassing having to explain to the emergency personnel what had happened, although they were very kind and let the kids sit in the fire truck while it was parked in the driveway. Her neighbor, hearing the commotion, came over to investigate and, sizing up the situation with an experienced mother's eye, invited the preschoolers over to play with her kids for the day so the new mom could lie down for a nap as soon as she got the baby back to sleep.

Yes, we moms have lots of stories to tell, assuming we live to tell them. Here are some of my favorite funnies; I hope that even after a sleepless night, they help make your mornings a little merrier.

Motherhood Mirth

THE FAMILY CIRCUS   **By Bil Keane**

"PJ's running away from home, but
he can't reach the doorknob."

You know you're a mother when . . .

- You can communicate two messages simultaneously: one while you talk on the phone and the other through vigorous hand signals.
- You've attuned your hearing to hear red Kool-Aid being spilled three rooms away.

- You can rattle off the names of everyone in the family, including the family pets, but not the name of the child standing directly in front of you.

☺

Out of the mouths of babes . . .
comes stuff we don't wanna see!

☺

THE FAMILY CIRCUS   **By Bil Keane**

"Can I have a cookie jar for
my room?"

☺

Mona, a South Carolina mom, shared this funny story with me.

Our family always sat at the back of the church, and when our daughter was little, she would run down the aisle when "children's church" was called. Kaelee loved to sit on the edge of the platform with the other kids and swing her legs real big while the lesson was presented.

One Sunday when Kaelee was three, she ran down to sit on the platform, as always. Because we were sitting in the back, we couldn't quite see what was happening, but as the children's lesson was given, a little wave of laughter moved through the congregation.

When we got home from church, I helped Kaelee change into her playclothes and was surprised to see that she wasn't wearing any underwear beneath her dress!

"Kaelee, where are your panties?" I asked.

"Where *are* my panties?" the perplexed Kaelee echoed.

It was then that I realized I had given Kaelee her dress, shoes, and socks to put on before church—but no panties. And *then* I remembered how Kaelee loved to swing her legs so high as she sat on the platform—and the twittering of laughter that had passed over the congregation during the children's sermon.

My mother was listening as I put two and two together. She laughed and said, "You all will have to move your membership!"

That night I saw the pastor's wife, and she laughed with me and said, "I didn't realize I needed to do panty checks on my girls before we started children's church!"[1]

☺

A baby is a loud noise at one end and no sense of responsibility at the other.[2]

☺

THE FAMILY CIRCUS.   By Bil Keane

"I'd like to leave a wake-up call for whenever it is I wake up."

☺

When three-year-old Olivia got upset with her mother, she appealed to a higher authority. No, not Grandma. She would tell her mother, rather huffily, "Mom, I'm just gonna have to talk to God about this."[3]

—SOURCE UNKNOWN

☺

I note with great interest that when God made the first human being, Adam, He created him as a complete adult and thus totally bypassed diapers, colic, toddlerhood, adolescence, and driving lessons. . . .

My personal theory is that God designed parenthood, in part, as an enormous character-building exercise, and since God does not personally require character improvement, He didn't need to bother getting Adam to eat strained peas.

—DAVE MEURER[4]

☺

There is nobody who is thirstier than a four-year-old who has just gone to bed.

—FRAN LEBOWITZ[5]

☺

I love the holiday one witty woman has proposed so stay-at-home moms can get a little rest. She calls it Please Take My Children to Work Day.[6]

☺

A local firefighter was teaching fire safety to three- and four-year-olds. One of his first questions was, "What do you do if your clothes are on fire?"

Instantly, one of the kids shouted out, "Close your closet door!"

—TIM BETE[7]

☺

The LORD lifts the fallen and those bent beneath their loads.

—PSALM 145:14 TLB

4

School-Age Live Wires
Carpooling to Problemville

*Y*ou might think when the kids head off to school, a mother's life would get a little easier. And in some ways it does. Now Mom has a few hours during the day for herself or her career—in between the kids' calls begging her to bring forgotten items to their class-room and the school's calls telling her that Johnny broke his finger playing dodge ball and needs to go to the emergency room.

But for those moms whose children's heads are filled with brain cells prone to forgetfulness, daydreaming, curiosity, imagination, thrill-seeking, or mischief-making —and isn't that just about all of us?—the school years seem to introduce a whole new era of exciting misad-ventures. These are the years when our kids seem to drift—or run headlong—into Problemville, and too often they seem to take the whole family, or the whole neighborhood, with them. These are the days and nights sprinkled with adrenaline-packed moments that linger on in a mother's memory long after her heart has stopped racing and her blood pressure has returned to normal.

Committed

Nonparents might smell a whiff of smoke, feel a drop of water falling from the first-floor ceiling, or hear a window opening and stay in that spot a moment longer, musing about the source. An experienced mom of school-age children, on the other hand, will spring instantly from her chair and seek out the scene of the crime, expecting to find someone playing with matches on the living room carpet, flooding the upstairs bathtub while attempting to bathe the cat, or coaxing a squirrel into the bedroom with peanut butter smeared on the windowsill.

Bracing for School-Age Surprises
This is the time in our lives when we answer the telephone and steel ourselves as the caller introduces herself: "Hello, Shirley, this is Margaret, across the street."

Our mothering instinct tells us something bad is coming, and sure enough, the next words we hear may be, "I thought you'd want to know that some boys are sitting on the roof of that empty house next door to you. One of them looks like your Toby. The good news is, it looks like they're doing their homework."

The next week it's Shirley's turn to call Margaret: "I thought you might want to know that some little girls are playing in that minivan parked in your driveway. One of them looks like your Abby. And I think I just heard the engine start up."

"Don't worry too much about this note . . .
the teacher was kind of angry when she wrote it."

When you're a mom of school-age kids, you may be happily tiptoeing through the tulips one minute and facedown in the dirt of despair the next. In one neighborhood, two moms were out walking on a Sunday afternoon, pleasantly chatting as they completed their workout. Then they turned the corner and spotted four police cars parked in front of an empty house on their block. Wondering what had happened, they came closer, only to find *their* sons, leaning into a wall, hands up, feet spread apart, while two of the officers patted them down! The boys had decided to check out the interior of the empty house on the very day the owner had decided to wait inside to see who had been breaking in.

One mom nearly had a heart attack when she came home from the grocery store and found her sixth-grade daughter bouncing sky-high on the backyard trampoline. Of course that, in itself, was nothing new. The problem was the little girl's companion on the trampoline: her new friend, the young daughter of a very successful personal-injury trial attorney who had just moved into the neighborhood. With terrifying visions of injuries, lawsuits, and homelessness, the woman quickly coaxed the girls off the trampoline and somehow persuaded them to come inside and play Uno.

THE FAMILY CIRCUS.   **By Bil Keane**

"Why is that silly man blowing his horn?"

Mischievous Career Indicators

At this age, children's clever imaginations often lead them into actions and antics that may give parents an indication of their future career choices. For example, one woman years ago overheard her young son and daughter playing in the backyard, digging trenches and building forts to guard against an attack by imaginary enemy agents they called "the diarrheas." Her son is now an engineer, and the daughter is enrolled in medical school.

Many enterprising school-age entrepreneurs set up lemonade stands; those with a more creative business sense have been known to add free giveaways from their dad's priceless baseball card collection as incentives to attract customers.

THE FAMILY CIRCUS   By Bil Keane

"Instead of a time-out, could I just pay a fine?"

One mom named Lisa described an incident when her six-year-old son, Matt, showed a host of talents that could lead him into a career as a Wal-Mart greeter, a marketing agent, or a funeral director. Matt was a live wire whose brain was always crackling with new ideas and adventures that kept his mom constantly on full alert.

Lisa, her husband, and their three kids, including young Matt, returned to their hometown and gathered with other family members for a funeral. It was a tragic situation, a heartbreaking loss for the family, but Matt found a way to insert a little sparkle of laughter into even that somber occasion.

During visitation at the funeral home, the family was standing in an informal receiving line, welcoming the friends and neighbors who had come to express their condolences. "I was standing there with my two older children when it suddenly occurred to me that Matt was nowhere in sight," Lisa said. "When a friend I knew came through the line, I asked, 'Have you seen Matt?'"

"He's standing at the front door, welcoming people," the friend answered.

Knowing Matt's reputation for doing and saying things that are, shall we say, out of the ordinary, Lisa hurried outside. And sure enough, there was Matt, politely holding the door open as people arrived, saying, "Welcome to the funeral home! Thanks for coming.

Please sign the book. If the page is filled up, please turn the page. Tips appreciated but not required."

By the time his mom got to him, Matt had $1.25 in his pocket. "I grabbed him by the ear and dragged him back inside," Lisa said.[1]

"I'm not saying kids today are over-protected, but *I* never had to wear a helmet to make toast!"

When Mama's Mind Goes Missing

For many of us moms of school-age kids, one of the most common stresses is the dreaded field trip, when parents are asked to help corral a group of school kids on a visit to a place that might be downright fun or interesting—if it wasn't crawling with a zillion kids, eight of whom might be the ones we were supposed to keep in sight and out of trouble every moment of the excursion.

A lot of things can go wrong on a field trip, and usually they're not the things you expect or plan for. One Florida mom was asked to drive a car behind the school bus when her child's class took a field trip to Epcot so that they would have a means of handling minor problems without, say, driving the whole busload of kids to K-Mart for replacements when Suzy lost her shoes somewhere on the water ride in the Norwegian exhibit.

DENNIS THE MENACE

"TIME TO GET UP. THIS GUY WANTS TO SEE THE LADY OF THE HOUSE."

Before they left the school, the teacher had given the group parents strict instructions: "Stay with your assigned kids at all times. You must be with them as soon as they step off the bus, and you must not let them out of your sight. We've had problems in the past with kids getting separated and lost, and believe me, it is *not* something we want to live through again. I think one of the mothers is still in therapy."

THE FAMILY CIRCUS **By Bil Keane**

"I'm grounded. I said one more word
to my mother."

So the mom happily followed the bus, thankful she didn't have to ride it, but when they arrived at Epcot, the buses were directed to one enormous parking lot and cars to another. With the teacher's instructions still ringing in her ears, she hurriedly parked her car while straining to keep "her" school bus in sight among the dozens of other buses meandering through the lots. Then she rushed across the vast pavement, found the right bus, and herded her kids into the park.

It was only when it was time to go that the awful truth hit her. She had been so focused on keeping the school bus in sight, she had no memory at all of where she had parked in the nine-thousand-space lot. Long after the school bus had gone home, she was still riding up and down the rows in a golf cart driven by a park employee, miserably trying to find her car. A couple of hours later, she finally remembered she had driven her husband's car that day.

And it's not only the moms who actually go on the field trips who have all the adventures. Sometimes the moms who stay behind incur nightmares too. For example, one girl who got car sick on the long bus ride threw up in her lunch bag during a field trip somewhere. She asked her group's mom to carry it around all day at the state capitol so that it didn't accidentally get thrown into the trash. You see, in the lunch bag, mixed with her uneaten sandwich and her regurgitated breakfast, was the thousand-dollar orthodontic appliance the girl's mother would have to dig out of the mess when the child finally got home!

There's even a story—I've often wondered if it could really be true—about a field trip to a small zoo, where the kids were given a special tour that included an up-close-and-personal visit with a cute young elephant. The animal's handler stood beside the gentle giant, inviting the students to touch the elephant's amazing trunk; they even got to feed it peanuts. As the zookeeper explained the elephant's habits, traits, and background, the day grew warmer, and one little boy shrugged off his nylon windbreaker and lifted it over the heads of his classmates to hand it to the group mom.

In a flash the elephant's trunk streaked out and grabbed the red windbreaker, shoved it into its mouth, and swallowed it. The kids shrieked, and the handler poked the elephant with his stick until it vomited up the jacket. Someone shoved it in a plastic bag, and it was delicately presented to the boy's mother later that afternoon. She wanted to throw it away, but her son persuaded her to wash it and give it back to him. "I'm the only kid in my class who has a jacket an elephant ate," he explained.

The mom was just glad it came out the *front* end of the elephant.

Oh, what memories are created as these fast-paced, excitement-filled school years fly by. If we're lucky, we'll live long enough to be able to laugh about them, once the smoke clears and the damage is repaired.

Motherhood Mirth

Most children threaten at times to run away from home. This is the only thing that keeps some parents going.

—PHYLLIS DILLER[2]

Little Billy was left to fix lunch. When his mother returned with a friend, she noticed that Billy had already strained the tea.

"Did you find the tea strainer?" his mother asked.

"No, Mother, I couldn't, so I used the fly swatter," replied Billy.

His mother nearly fainted, so Billy hastily added, "Don't get excited, Mother. I used an old one."[3]

☺

T-ball players do get distracted at times. During one game, a player pointed toward center field as he took the plate. At first it appeared he was imitating Babe Ruth, showing the fans where he was going to hit a home run. Then I heard the sound of the ice cream truck passing by. The entire team turned and started walking—as if in a trance —toward the truck. All, except for the second baseman who was writing his name in the dirt, and the first baseman who was trying to catch a butterfly, and the right fielder who was practicing his somersaults.[4]

"I promised my teacher I'd bring in your small intestine for my Science Fair project!"

(The source of the funny items that follow is unknown.)

Things you'll probably never hear a mother say:

"Just leave all the lights on—we have extra money this month for the electric bill."

"Let me smell that shirt. Yeah, it's good for another week."

"Go ahead and keep that stray dog, honey; I'll be glad to take care of it for you."

"Well, if Timmy's mom says it's OK, that's good enough for me!"

"The curfew is just a general time to shoot for—give or take three or four hours."

"You don't need a tissue; just wipe your nose on your sleeve."

"Don't bother wearing a jacket. The windchill is bound to improve."

☺

Phenomena mothers have learned from their children:

- A king-size waterbed holds enough water to fill a two-thousand-square-foot house four inches deep.
- A ceiling fan can hit a baseball a long way.
- The glass in windows doesn't stop a baseball hit by a ceiling fan.
- When you hear the commode flush and the words "uh-oh," it's already too late.
- Marbles in gas tanks make lots of noise when driving.

- The spin cycle on the washing machine does not make earthworms dizzy. It will, however, make cats dizzy.
- Cats throw up twice their body weight when dizzy.

☺

After two consecutive snow days, the mothers of Curdleyville storm the superintendent's house.

☺

In Him all things hold together.

—COLOSSIANS 1:17 NASB

5

Adolescents and Teens

How My Hair Turned Gray

*F*or a dozen years or so, your kids think you are the world's greatest creation. You can meet them at the bus stop wearing old sweatpants and your husband's stained T-shirt, and they scamper into your arms excitedly telling you about their adventures as though they'd been away in the Hundred Years' War. Then comes the morning when they show up at the breakfast table and you bend down for the usual good-morning kiss only to hear, "Really, Mom! I'm not a baby anymore. So could you knock it off with the baby kisses? Just leave me alone, will ya!"

In case you're the mother of sweet, adorable toddlers right now, I share this information, not to scare you, but to prepare you—and to offer some reassurance. It's just a stage. In all likelihood, your children will get through this turbulent passage unscarred and come out the other side of it with their normal, pleasant personality intact. I'm sorry I can't promise the same thing for you. But with any luck at all, they'll remember to visit you occasionally in the Home for the Bewildered.

Copyright 2002 by Randy Glasbergen.
www.glasbergen.com

SPENDING = GROWTH
GROWTH = JOBS
JOBS = SECURITY
SECURITY = HAPPINESS

"...and *that's* why you need to raise my allowance!"

If you're just now entering this stage, you probably need to start practicing some flexibility exercises so you can keep up with your adolescent and teenage children's mood swings. During the next few years, you'll probably find yourself occasionally being the focus of great adoration and thoughtfulness one minute (when your seventh-grader is trying to sweet-talk you into buying the latest video game, for instance) and incredulous outrage the next (when you explain that no, he can't have a two-year advance on his allowance).

If your children are like most who pass through this stage, they are discovering thrilling new emotions and characteristics—especially sarcasm and stupidity. They like nothing better than to use these intriguing discoveries to trigger explosions of hysterics in their frazzled mothers—to whom they say such things as, "Calm down, Mom. I only drove through the garage door. It's not like I knocked down the whole house."

© 2004 Randy Glasbergen. www.glasbergen.com

"Actually, I only come here to lie down.
I can't get any rest at home!"

My advice: brace yourself for the calamities, enjoy the lulls between crises, and laugh about everything you possibly can. Finally, seek out a good therapist . . . and *pray*.

Surely You're Not Wearing *That!*

Many kids develop a unique sense of fashion during these years. Mothers of daughters often have the most difficult time in this stage. One day their little princesses are decked out in frilly dresses and Mary Jane shoes— and the next morning they emerge from their bedrooms wearing too-tiny tank tops, micro-miniskirts, army boots, and black lipstick.

And just as they're outfitting themselves in clothes that would give the Victorians a heart attack, they're also becoming more aware of their mothers' appalling lack of fashion sense. For instance, one of the biggest disagreements about clothing styles worn by teens and their parents right now concerns just where the waistband should touch the body. While many baby boomers are happy wearing slacks and skirts that have a waistband worn at the actual waist, the younger set prefers the low-slung style that makes the rest of us believe in miracles. (The miracle being that those low-riding clothes don't fall right down to the kids' ankles every time they move.)

SPEED BUMP — By Dave Coverly

IF KIDS THESE DAYS ARE SO MUCH FATTER, WHY ARE THEIR BRITCHES ALWAYS SLIDING DOWN?..

© 2006 Dave Coverly. Used by permission of Dave Coverly.

Driving Doozies

Kids also develop a new sense of propriety at this stage about what is and is not acceptable transportation. Suddenly the kid whose mom drives a minivan asks her to let him out at the corner instead of dropping him off in front of the school. But as soon as these kids get a driver's license of their own there's no telling what kind of vehicle they may fall in love with.

Our son Tim drove a little Volkswagen bug with a giant wind-up key attached to the back. And our son

Steve drove . . . a hearse. I know it sounds strange, but once again, I have to admit that I was in on the fun. As Steve and I were driving home from church one Sunday we went by a car lot where a big, black Cadillac hearse was for sale for only $350 (this was decades ago, but even then it was quite a bargain).

"Wow!" Steve exclaimed. "Wouldn't it be great to have something like *that*?"

*"Mother . . . please tell me this isn't you
in these hideous bell-bottoms."*

Taken from *Motherhood Is Stranger Than Fiction* by Mary Chambers. © 1995 by Mary Chambers. Used by permission of InterVarsity Press. P.O. Box 1400, Downers Grove, IL 60515. www.ivpress.com .

Steve hadn't had his driver's license too long, and I'm sure he never dreamed that I would consider buying the hearse. But we stopped and talked to the salesman and checked out the huge vehicle. The interior was lined with beautiful purple velvet, and there was a compartment near the back that held a shovel and a spade. For Steve, it was love at first sight.

Bill had already driven home from church with our other boys, and I made a snap decision and wrote out a check to buy the hearse. Steve could hardly contain himself as he drove it home.

When we got there, Bill could hardly contain himself, either—but not out of glee. It took some fast talking to get him to let Steve keep the hearse. We really couldn't afford it at the time because Bill was still recovering from a severe car crash that had nearly left him in a lifelong vegetative state, so we had lots of bills and little income. But we needed some fun in our lives— and the hearse was a lot of fun, indeed.

Steve's friends were enthralled with the hearse. They wanted to sit in it, drive it, and even try out the shovel and spade. It only got six miles to the gallon, but being a good businessman, Steve managed to make a few dollars by renting it to some of his buddies for Halloween. They decorated it and had a great time driving it around, haunting the neighborhood. I still have photos of that Halloween night, as well as pictures of Steve and his friends heading for the beach in his hearse, their surfboards hanging out the back.

"Relax mom...it's macaroni."

In addition to his little Volkswagen, Tim drove a hearse too, a pink one. Well, it wasn't really his, and it wasn't really pink—at least he insisted it wasn't. It belonged to the mortuary where he had a part-time job for a while (a company that was known for its "rose-colored" vehicles). Our firstborn son was a serious, conscientious young man who, like many kids his age, developed a rather warped sense of humor. While Steve thought it would be fun to drive a hearse, Tim thought it would be fun to work for a funeral home. What can I say?

Tim's idea of doing something hilarious was to bring home bows from the funeral bouquets and decorate our dogs or our cat with "Rest in Peace" or "God Bless Grandpa Hiram." (During a talk I gave somewhere several years ago, I told about Tim's bringing home the bows from the mortuary for the dogs and cat, and a darling little old lady came up afterward and said, "Mrs. Johnson, I feel so bad to think your son brought home the bones from the mortuary." I tried to reassure her that Tim had never brought home any bones—only *bows*.)

Tim would sometimes stop at home while on duty and have lunch, leaving the hearse parked in the driveway. One day he took his little brother Barney to the mortuary. Making sure no one was around, Tim let Barney climb into an empty casket in the sales room, just to see what it felt like. Then (just for fun), Tim shut the lid! (I told you he had a warped sense of humor!)

Barney let out a yelp, and Tim opened the lid in a few seconds—after he had enjoyed a good laugh at Barney's expense, of course.

No surprise, Barney blabbed when he got home, and I gave Tim a lecture about the dangers of closing up his brother in a casket. "You could scar him for life!" I warned. (You never know what kind of lectures you're going to be called upon to give your kids, do you?)

"I'm forming a support group for women who feel overwhelmed by cooking, children, and housework. We meet every weeknight from 5:00 to 10:00 PM."

The next day Barney went to school and blabbed again, telling his classmates about what had happened.

Barney's teacher listened to his incredible tale and later phoned me to say, "Mrs. Johnson, I don't like to tell you this, but I'm afraid Barney is starting to tell lies. He's coming up with stories that just *can't* be true!"

When she told me what Barney had said, I assured her that, unfortunately, Barney *wasn't* lying and that the story was true. "His big brother just has a different sense of humor," I said with a nervous chuckle. I'm not sure I totally convinced her.

Now, this is a book about humor, and I don't want to steal any of the joy out of the fun we're having. But while I'm talking about Tim and Steve and their lively antics and crazy cars, I need to say how grateful I am for these zany memories, because now that's all I have left of these two precious sons. Steve was killed in Vietnam, and five years later, Tim was killed in a car crash caused by a drunk driver in Yukon Territory, Canada, as he was driving home from Alaska. Yes, I've learned the hard way to laugh every chance I get so I'll have sweet memories to cherish during any dark days that may lie ahead.

Brace for Impact

For many parents, the funniest—and potentially the most terrifying—memories originate during those nail-biter days when our teenagers are learning to drive. Few things are more challenging than sitting in the passenger seat while a brand-new driver confidently assures us, "Relax, Mom. I know what I'm doing."

One mom of two teenagers said she thought her arms had permanently frozen in the "brace position" after spending two consecutive years riding in the passenger seat beside her learner's-permit drivers. During one hair-raising episode, she said, they were riding down a two-lane highway on the outskirts of town. Her fifteen-year-old son, who had gotten his permit the week before, was at the wheel, and his fourteen-year-old sister was in the backseat.

"Looks like another case of PTKD paralysis—
Parent Teaching Kid to Drive."

"I knew there was a produce stand up ahead, so I gave Marcus plenty of warning that I wanted to stop there," she recalled. "Several cars were coming toward us in the other lane, and Marcus apparently didn't want to have to wait for them to pass before he could turn, so he abruptly swung the steering wheel to the left, barely missing the oncoming traffic. When I opened my eyes, we were sailing down the left-side shoulder with cars whizzing by us on our right and a train rolling beside us on the tracks to our left. It all made me dizzy, and I just kept screaming and closed my eyes again."

The produce stand—and a light pole—were still about a quarter-mile ahead. And while Marcus's two terrified passengers braced for impact, Marcus calmly cruised full-speed down the left-hand shoulder, missing the light pole by inches. Finally he skidded to a stop right in front of the tomato bin, enveloping the business and its customers in a storm cloud of dust and gravel. It was, said the mom, one of the most spectacular arrivals ever made at that quiet little countryside business.

Whether you're gliding smoothly through this segment of the motherhood highway—or screaming your lungs out in the passenger seat—I hope that somehow you'll find a way to have fun and enjoy the ride. Someday, if your mind is still intact when the dust settles, you can look back on this challenging time and cherish the memories you've shared with your kids during their adolescent and teenage years.

Motherhood Mirth

Life Classes for Teenagers
Some mothers are urging schools to include in their curricula special courses that help students apply scientific principles to everyday life. Here are some of the classes that have been proposed.

How to Close the Refrigerator Door: *Cool lessons on how hinges operate*

Floors and Laundry Hampers: How to Tell the Difference: *Slide presentation with handouts*

Floors and Laundry Hampers (advanced): General Function and Use: *Exciting, hands-on opportunities to transmogrify dirty clothes from one to the other* (Related topic: Trash cans and How They Operate)

Mold and Fungus 101 (rated R; not recommended for the squeamish): The Monster Living under Your Bed in Last Month's Pizza Box: *Aromatherapy-enhanced slide show.*

Amazing Financial Secrets: Accepting the Fact That Your Mom Is Not an ATM: *Learn the two little words that put money in your pocket:* earn it

Relationships: Would It Kill You to Take Your Little Sister to the Movies Once in a While? *Amazing stories of performing and surviving an act of kindness*

☺

In his book, *Nelson's Big Book of Laughter*, Lowell Streiker shares this story from his neighbor Marie:

> Late one Saturday evening I was awakened by the ringing of my phone. In a sleepy, grumpy voice, I said, "Hello."
>
> The party on the other end of the line paused for a moment before rushing breathlessly into a lengthy speech. "Mom, this is Susanna and I'm sorry I woke you up, but I had to call because I'm going to be a little late getting home. See, Dad's car has a flat, but it's not my fault. Honest! I don't know what happened. The tire just went flat while we were inside the theater. Please don't be mad, okay?"
>
> Since I don't have any daughters, I knew the person had misdialed. "I'm sorry, dear," I replied, "but I have to tell you you've reached the wrong number. I don't have a daughter named Susanna. In fact, I don't have any daughter at all."
>
> A pause. "Gosh, Mom," came the young woman's quavering voice, "I didn't think you'd be this mad."[1]

☺

There's nothing wrong with teenagers that reasoning with them won't aggravate.[2]

☺

Bizarro

It's common at your age to hate your body. But as you get older, you learn instead to hate other people's.

☺

Q: How many exhausted mothers of teenagers does it take to change a lightbulb?

A: Just one. All by herself. She changes the lightbulbs *and* the toilet tissue rolls *and* the sheets, *and* she changes the clocks in the fall and in the spring. And she does it without ANY HELP from ANYBODY, and do you know *WHY*? Because NOBODY in this house ever lifts a finger to help with ANYTHING ANYTIME ANYWHERE. If anything *does* get changed around here, you can just FORGET ASKING ANY OF THE TEENAGERS TO HELP, FOR HEAVEN'S SAKE because they are

TOO BUSY with their ALL-IMPORTANT VIDEO GAMES and THEIR TELEPHONE CALLS and their all-important INSTANT MESSAGING. Don't even THINK about asking them to DO SOMETHING HELPFUL, LIKE CHANGING A LIGHTBULB OR, EVEN MORE RIDICULOUS, TAKING OUT THE TRASH. Good old MOM does all the changing around here, and she's done it EVER SINCE SHE CHANGED THEIR DIA-PERS, and they didn't appreciate her then, and they certainly DON'T APPRECIATE HER NOW. And if, by some chance, she FELL OFF THE CHAIR AND BROKE HER NECK while she was changing the stupid light-bulb, DO YOU THINK ANYONE WOULD NOTICE? NOT A CHANCE! In fact, THEY WOULD STEP OVER HER COLD, BROKEN BODY AND SAY, "GEEZ, YOU'D THINK SHE'D PUT THE CHAIR AWAY WHEN SHE WAS FINISHED."

☺

Oh, to be half as wonderful as my child thought I was—and only half as stupid as my teenager thinks I am.[3]

☺

Covert Conversation Rule: If you don't want your children to hear what you are saying, pretend you're talking to them.[4]

☺

© 1996 Randy Glasbergen.
www.glasbergen.com

"I spoke with a social worker today. If you
keep playing 70's music, they're going to
put me in a foster home."

☺

Raising teenagers is like trying to nail Jell-O to the wall.

☺

He gives strength to the weary
    and increases the power of the weak.
Even youths grow tired and weary,
    and young men stumble and fall;
but those who hope in the LORD
    will renew their strength.
They will soar on wings like eagles;
    they will run and not grow weary,
    they will walk and not be faint.

—ISAIAH 40:29–31

6

Parenting Adults

I Don't Care How Old You Are, I'm Still Your Mother!

*P*arents have different reactions when their kids graduate from high school and head off into the future. Some moms and dads go through a period of mourning, grieving over the quiet emptiness of their home. Others go through a period of partying, celebrating a return to the freedom they enjoyed in the days before they had kids.

Either way, mothering continues despite the distance that separates us from our children, whether it's across town or across the country. But for many of us it shifts into a different mode, one that focuses less on hands-on time and discipline and more on communication—and prayer.

The way I see it, God gives us our children, and while

they're in our homes, we are His hands on earth, doing everything we can to raise up those kids in the way He has taught us. For eighteen years or so, it's His guidance but our hands in the hands-on operation.

When our children move out and leave our daily control, we have to put them back into God's hands, knowing that He loves them even more than we do. And in the case of kids who've put us through a particularly rambunctious term of teenagery, we might warn Him, "Lord, You're gonna have some problems with this one!"

A Mother's Mantra

As many of us moms know so well, adult children living on their own can make some pretty poor decisions and act out in crazy ways. But if your kids are adults and living away from home, they have to take responsibility for their own decisions and actions. Keep telling yourself this! And remember what I've said to hurting parents now for nearly thirty years: where there's no control, there's no responsibility. If your kid makes a mistake, you can offer hope, help, and encouragement. Just don't blame yourself for his or her problems.

Moms will always worry; it's in our makeup to do so. But we also pray and trust God to watch over our kids and give us strength to handle whatever may happen in the future. That's how we keep the worries from consuming us. We still want to know everything that's going on in our children's lives (well, maybe not *everything*), and we try to help them as much as we can without overstepping our new role as the mother of adults. It's a delicate balancing act, this role of mothering adults without meddling, and it's hard to know if we're leaning the right way. Let's face it: sometimes we just can't help ourselves.

Giving in to Meddling
One time our son David came for Easter dinner, and on his drive back to his condo (he lived about an hour away), he stopped to buy gasoline before he got on the freeway. While he was pumping the gas, the nozzle

went crazy and wouldn't shut off. "Mom, by the time I finally got it stopped, gas was everywhere—in my hair, my eyes, and all over the new sweater you gave me," he told me in a phone call when he finally got home.

Horrified to hear what had happened, I asked, "What did you do?"

"I went into the men's room, took off the sweater, and decided it was ruined; I just threw it in the trash barrel," he said. "My pants were soaked with gas too, but I couldn't exactly throw them away and drive home naked!"

Thankful that he had made it home safely, I couldn't help but obsess about that sweater. I had bought it at Knott's Berry Farm as a Christmas present for David, and I knew he loved it because he had it on nearly every time I saw him. I hated to think of it wadded up and wasted in some gas-station trash barrel.

So . . . (if you're a mother, you probably already know what I did next, don't you?) . . . I grabbed a plastic trash bag and jumped in the car. I drove the route I thought David had taken and stopped at every gas station between our house and the freeway, asking the attendant at each one if I could check the trash in the men's restroom! At the *eighth* one, I found it—and it *was* soaked with gasoline. Even with it tied up in the plastic bag, my car was filled with fumes by the time I got back home. Bill was in the driveway when I pulled up, and when I showed him the sweater, he said, "For Pete's sake, don't bring it in the house. Just leave it outside, and it'll air out."

So I spread it over some lawn furniture and left it there overnight, and believe it or not (remember, I live in Southern California, where it rarely rains), that night it poured. The next morning I wrung out as much moisture as I could, then I washed it repeatedly in Woolite. It came out as good as new! I excitedly packed it up and mailed it to David, tucking in some tissues sprinkled with Bill's Royal Copenhagen aftershave for good measure.

I could hardly wait to hear from my grateful son, telling me how brilliant I was for finding and restoring his sweater and how happy he was to have it back. But that call never came. I started to wonder if the sweater had gotten lost in the mail. It even occurred to me that David had gotten the sweater but felt embarrassed to have realized his mother had followed his trail and dug through men's-room trash cans in all those gas stations. Or—of course it was a ridiculous, farfetched idea, but *could he have thought I was meddling?*

Finally, a week later, I couldn't stand it any longer. I would be going near David's condo as I drove to and from a women's retreat I would be attending over the weekend. I left a message on his answering machine saying I would stop by on my way home to take him to lunch. That Sunday I rang his doorbell, and David threw open the door. There he stood in his favorite sweater, a huge smile on his face as he flung out his arms and said, "Smell me, Mom! Smell me!"

"That *is* an impressive Spring Break party, sweetie. That reminds me, your mother requests you no longer be honest with us"

© Philpott/McCammon/Used by permission

Bittersweet Emotions

Yes, things change when our kids grow into adults and move out. The utility bills go down, the long-distance bills go up, and our role as mothers evolves when our children move into homes of their own. We wipe tears from our eyes when our college freshman calls home, homesick and miserable, and we celebrate when the happy call comes that he or she has passed that first big exam and made some new friends. We encourage our job-seeking sons and daughters and stand in anxious pride when our determined adult children graduate from military training. And we try not to scream when they come home for the first time after happily having themselves pierced or tattooed. Oh, the emotions we mothers feel as our babies head off into the great beyond.

"I'LL BET HIS MOM IS GONNA TAKE AWAY
ALL OF HIS MARKERS."

Trusting God for Miracles, Small and Large
Somewhere I read a comment that mothers continually watch their children, even as adults, hoping for any

small sign of improvement. When we see that their minds have matured and their hearts have softened and become more receptive, we can't help but rejoice—and start to think maybe we did a better job of mothering than we first thought!

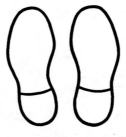

MOM'S HISSY-FIT FLOORMAT

Directions: When the need for throwing a hissy fit is felt, place both feet on the space provided and jump rapidly up and down. Incoherent screaming is also permissible. If symptoms persist, repeat as necessary until your children leave home. Or see your nearest psychiatrist. You *may* be a nut.

© 2006 Barbara Johnson

One mom shared the story of an adult daughter who went through an especially difficult period when, as the mom said, "If I were lying in the aisle, dying, she would have stepped right over me and gone on her way."

But the woman stayed strong in her faith, and she

kept praying that God would give her daughter a "teachable spirit." She also kept remembering how her heavenly Father "loves me no matter what I do," and she vowed to do the same for her daughter. "I know God is faithful, and I kept praying and kept my focus on Him," she said. "He gives us miracles every day, sometimes in the smallest ways, if we can just recognize them."

Eventually her relationship with her daughter was restored, and last year they went on a trip together. "We rented a two-bedroom condo at the beach, but my daughter came in and slept with me so we could stay close to each other," she said. "We talked and laughed and had a wonderful time."

This year they went back to the beach, "but this time we just got the one-bedroom condo," she said with a laugh.[1]

Coping with Heartache and Craziness

Like this mom, I've been through some difficult times and lived to laugh about them—some of them anyway. I know the agony that comes with the death of a child; I've gone through it twice. I also know the heartache of being alienated from an adult child, and I've felt the ecstatic joy of having that relationship restored. Along the way, in the books I've written, I've shared my own experiences in coping with excruciating circumstances and hair-raising situations, and other mothers' responses to those books have introduced me to a whole new world of problems I never knew existed.

It turns out that moms all over the world have gone through equally heartrending times with their adult children and lived to tell about them. Sometimes when they contact me they feel as though they're barely alive, but they're hanging in there—hanging on to hope. How thankful I am that God has blessed me with the gift of helping many of them learn to do what they thought was impossible: laugh again.

As you might expect, the death of our two sons threw me into the darkest period of my life, but that difficult time also included another excruciating ordeal. The day after our third son, David, graduated with honors from junior college, I accidentally discovered a drawer full of homosexual magazines in his bedroom. Suddenly I felt as though all the air had been sucked out of the room—and the breath had been sucked out of me. I couldn't believe what I was seeing. Couldn't believe *my* son could be interested in such horrifying (to me, at least) material.

Later that day I confronted him, and he admitted that he was homosexual. "Or," he said, "maybe bisexual."

I've joked many times since then that, in those days so long ago, I was naïve and hardly knew anything about homosexuality; I'd never even heard of anyone being *bisexual*. I didn't know what it was but wondered if it could mean sex twice a month!

David and I argued, and I said things I soon regretted. Afterward, to make a long story short (it's spelled out in my earlier books, especially *Stick a Geranium in Your Hat and Be Happy*), David disappeared, and during the next eleven years there were times when I didn't know if he was alive or dead.

I was mired in misery for a long time after David left. But eventually I gained the strength and trust to say, "Whatever, Lord!" knowing that God would keep me wrapped in His comfort blanket of love through whatever was to come. What He did for me was nothing short of miraculous. He filled my broken heart with the most amazing bubble of joy, an attitude that has carried me through some turbulent times and unbelievable obstacles since then. Most recently, those trials have included a malignant brain tumor and the death of my husband, Bill. But I'm still here, still trusting God, still lifted each day by that amazing bubble of joy.

In the last thirty or so years, I've talked with thousands of heartbroken moms whose children have died or whose adult kids have taken wrong turns and made crazy decisions. The main advice I give those hurting mothers is that all *they* can do is love their kids. Remember, if there's no control, there's no responsibility, and at this point only God can change them. So just love them unconditionally, the way God loves us when we make mistakes. That doesn't mean you have to let them move back in and upset the rest of the family. But they need to know your love is constant.

I recall telling David before he disappeared, "I can't change your life, but there are two things I can do for you—love you and pray for you. And until they close the casket over my head and put a lily in my hand, I'm going to do just that. Just remember—we love you unconditionally, and the porch light is always on for you."

My words didn't stop him from leaving; he was gone for years. But I like to think that eventually they brought him back to me. At any rate, he did come back, our relationship was restored, and today he is not only my son but my close friend and comforter.

Putting Things in Perspective

I haven't forgotten, though, how difficult it was to get through the years of estrangement. The death of my sons and the alienation from David certainly put into perspective any of the other "minor" parenting problems I'd had before. Yes indeed! We moms who know what it's like to be knocked senseless by tragedy can't help but laugh now at the things that used to send us into orbit:

"Like my hair, Mom? It's 'napalm green.'"

"I'm getting an F in history."

"I dented the fender."

"I lost your credit card."

"I burned the cake and incinerated the kitchen, but the rest of the house is still standing."

"I'm moving out."

"I'm moving back home."

As bad as they were at the time, those formerly disastrous announcements seem pretty tame to many of us now. Of course, we're different people than we were then. That was back when our lives seemed peaceful and our families were normal.

Now we're thankful if we can manage to have one moment of peace, and we haven't felt normal for a long, long time.

We've been through the wringer.

We've walked through the fire (that aroma we wear is the smoky scent of lingering disaster).

We've crawled our way through the tunnel (some of us are still groping through the darkness).

But in the trials we've faced, something good has happened too: God has fine-tuned us so we are more compassionate, more caring, more loving, more aware of others' pain. We have what I call credentials for sharing. They enable us to come alongside a mom who has recently fallen into life's cesspools and offer her a lifeline of hope. Just by sharing our credentials and showing her we're still standing, still breathing, we can encourage her to hold on, reminding her that what God has done for us, He can do for her. Then we can share with her that other amazing blessing, the gift of laughter.

Motherhood Mirth

(Except where noted, the sources of the following quips and jokes are unknown.)

☺

When Jesus said, "In this world you will have trouble," He wasn't kidding! (See John 16:33.)

☺

We've all heard of the twelve-step program, but have you ever heard of the *one*-step regimen?

"*WHAM!* Get over it!"

☺

If you treat every situation as a life-and-death matter ... you will die a lot.

☺

INSTRUCTIONS:
As bad news approaches,
flash this sign.

☺

Just when your kids are fit to live with,
they're living with someone else.

☺

The secret of dealing successfully with a child is not to be its parents.

☺

Remember that parents are supposed to give their kids road maps, but they don't have to pave the road for them.

☺

Creative Ways to Handle Stress
1. Forget the diet and send yourself a candy gram.
2. Put a paper bag on your head and mark it "Closed for remodeling."
3. Brush your teeth vigorously with Cheez Whiz.
4. Pound your head repeatedly on a pile of lightly toasted Wonder Bread.
5. Sit in your car and point your hairdryer at oncoming traffic like it's a radar gun.

☺

I am an old man and have known a great many troubles, but most of them never happened.

—MARK TWAIN

☺

The best exercise for good relationships:
bending over backward.

☺

A mother's prayer:
Lord, when I am wrong, make me willing to change.
And when I am right, make me easy to live with.

☺

But as for me, I will always have hope.

—PSALM 71:14

Notes

Chapter 1. Introduction: Just Do What I Tell You, and Nobody'll Get Hurt

1. Thanks to Jan Broadhead-Atkinson for sharing this witty line.

Chapter 2. Pregnancy and Birth: Sure They're Cute, but Having a Baby Is a Pain

1. Vicki Cheng, "Expectant Moms Discovering Hypnosis," *Tampa Tribune*, July 3, 2005, Baylife 9, reprinted from the *Raleigh* (NC) *News & Observer*.

2. Thanks to Kathleen Young for sharing this story.

3. From *Fatherhood* by Bill Cosby, copyright © 1986 by William H. Cosby, Jr. Used by permission of Doubleday, a division of Random House, Inc.

4. Paul Reiser, Babyhood (New York: william Morrow, 1997), 78. Reprinted with permission of HarperCollins

Chapter 3. Newborns and Toddlers: How a Mother Spells Relief: S-L-E-E-P

1. Thanks to Mona Ivy for sharing this story.

2. Ronald Knox, quoted in Geoff Tibballs, ed., *The Mammoth Book of Zingers, Quips, and One-Liners* (New York: Carroll & Graf/Avalon Publishing Group, 2004), 59. Appears by permission of the publisher, Carroll & Graf, A Division of Avalon Publishing Group, Inc.

3. Thanks to Karen Braswell for sharing this story.

4. Dave Meurer, *Boyhood Daze: An Incomplete Guide to Raising Boys* (Grand Rapids, Mich.: fleming H. Revell, a division of Baker Publishing Group, 1999), 13.

5. Fran Lebowitz, quoted in Tibballs, *Zingers, Quips and One-liners*, 107. Appears by permission of the publisher, Carroll & Graf, A Division of Avalon Publishing Group, Inc.

6. For details about the holiday Jennifer Singer is proposing, see her Website www.MommaSaid.net.

7. Excerpted from *In the Beginning . . . There Were No Diapers* by Tim Bete, © 2005. Used with permission of the publisher, Sorin Books, an imprint of Ave Maria Press, P.O. Box 428, Notre Dame, IN 46556, www.avemariapress.com.

Chapter 4. *School-Age Live Wires:* Carpooling to Problemville
1. Thanks to Lisa Martin for sharing this story.

2. Phyllis Diller, quoted in Tibballs, ed., *Zingers, Quips and One-Liners*, 106. Appears by permission of the publisher, Carroll & Graf, A Division of Avalon Publishing Group, Inc.

3. Taken from *World's Greatest Collection of Good Clean Jokes.* Copyright © 1998 Bob Phillips. Published by Harvest House Publishers, Eugene, OR. Used by permission. www.harvesthousepublishers.com

4. Excerpted from *In the Beginning . . . There Were No Diapers* by Tim Bete, © 2005. Used with permission of the publisher, Sorin Books, an imprint of Ave Maria Press, P.O. Box 428, Notre Dame, IN 46556, www.avemariapress.com.

Chapter 5. *Adolescents and Teens:* How My Hair Turned Gray
1. Lowell Streiker, *Nelson's Big Book of Laughter* (Nashville: Thomas Nelson, 2000), 417.

2. Ibid., 418.

3. Charlie "T." Jones and Bob Phillips, *Wit & Wisdom* (Eugene, Or.: Harvest House, 1977), 137.

4. Paul Dickson, *The Official Rules at Home* (New York: Walker, 1996), 24.

Chapter 6. *Parenting Adults:* I Don't Care How Old You Are, I'm Still Your Mother!
1. Thanks to Linda Wilson for sharing this story.

CPSIA information can be obtained at www.ICGtesting.com
Printed in the USA
LVOW10s1121290713

345142LV00006B/30/P